Swedish Body Massage Course

Swedish Body
TRAINING MANUAL

VTCT, ITEC, CITY & GUILDS, BABTAC, THE GUILD & FHT

Heated and Holistic Bamboo Massage, Holistic Massage, Swedish Body Massage, Reflexology, Professional Skincare and Facials. With all BABTAC accreditations, with upgrades to VTCT Level 3 or NVQ Units if required.

The Angel Academy of Teaching & Training
Loughton
Essex
IG10 4QN
www.angel-academy.co.uk
info@angel-academy.co.uk

© The AATT

Swedish Body Massage Course

THE ANGEL ACADEMY OF TEACHING AND TRAINING

The Angel Academy of Teaching and Training, Loughton, Essex are 'passionate' about teaching and training their students.

The school was founded in 2003 after its founder Deborah Kelly had spent many years in a high profile career which detailed National Press, Magazines, Radio and Terrestrial and Sky Television.

The fast pace of a responsible job in media was incredibly stressful and one full of media executives who had emotional breakdowns, stress and early heart attacks.

Following alongside her busy work schedule Deborah set out to train in 33 therapies and was approached by the Principle of a College to teach a range of Therapies. She completed her Teacher Training Units and Assessor Awards and begun to teach at many colleges as well as part-founding a centre in Harley Street, London in 1989. She is a qualified tutor for ITEC, VTCT, IIHHT, BABTAC, FHT and the CMA.

Deborah also founded a Teaching and Training School called the Angel Academy in 2003 to cater for students who required a high level of training for a competitive price.

During her extensive years of experience, she has worked with many celebrities, has been on set whilst films were being shot on location, and has worked privately with a supermodel and a highly acclaimed sportsman.

Over the years, Deborah has worked hard to find a team who will be as loyal and dedicated to the industry as her, who will be perfectionists in all they do and will seek to always work to the highest standard.

We hope that you will enjoy being taught as much as we will enjoy teaching you. It makes us the happiest of all to know that our students will go on to receive certificates of excellence.

© The AATT

Swedish Body Massage Course

HEALTH AND SAFETY IN THE WORKPLACE

The Angel Academy of Teaching and Training is committed to providing a safe environment and will:

1. Provide guidance on safe working practices for staff and students.

2. Incorporate health and safety knowledge into all student activities.

3. Provide information, procedures and equipment for fire and emergencies.

4. Provide information, procedures and equipment for accidents.

5. Provide training and up-to-date information on health and safety to all concerned.

Promote a responsible attitude to health and safety throughout the centre.

The Angel Academy of Teaching and Training will ensure that its students:

1. Observe the centre's health and safety regulations.

2. Co-operate with others in keeping the environment safe.

3. Take care to avoid injury to themselves or others by being appropriately dressed and not misusing or causing damage to equipment, materials or the premises.

4. Report any hazard to the tutor in charge or other responsible person immediately.

The Angel Academy of Teaching and Training will carry out Risk Assessment:

3

© The AATT

Swedish Body Massage Course

This evaluation will be carried out prior to any new course taking place. A risk assessment will allow the school to take precautions to minimise the likelihood of an incident/accident from taking place. A form will carry the following information for each course:

1.   What are the hazards

2.   Who might be harmed

3.   What precautions have been taken to reduce the likelihood of harm

4.   What further action is necessary

5.   Risk Assessment Priority

6.   Review date as and where applicable

Swedish Body Massage Course

FIRST AID IN THE WORKPLACE

A list of First- Aid qualified Tutors should be made available to each Student. Students will be shown where the First-Aid box is located should it be required. On this occasion, the first point of contact for reporting an accident/incident should be head Tutor and First-Aid qualified: Mrs Deborah Kelly

The Health and Safety Work Act Of 1974

This covers the VR74 and VR02 health and safety units covered for VTCT. A health and Safety Inspector regularly visits the School to observe the following:

1.   An up to date PAT test on all electrical equipment

2.   Potential hazards are identified

3.   All incidents are recorded

4.   COSHH

5.   Any spillages are cleared safely

6.   Tutors to be trained in first aid

7.   RIDDOR

8.   Safe working environment

RIDDOR- Reporting Injuries, Diseases and Occurrences 1985 Act

The Angel Academy of Teaching and Training is responsible for reporting any Injuries, Diseases or occurrences to the Head of School: Mrs Deborah Kelly.

All incidents must be recorded in an accident report book, where the staff member and/or student signs the report.

I cases of major injury, a local health inspector or the environmental health officer should be advised.

© The AATT

Swedish Body Massage Course

COSHH- The Control of Hazardous substances according to Health Regulations 1988 Act

The Angel Academy of Teaching and Training is responsible for the control of potentially hazardous substances by storing them correctly using the following methods:

1.   All containers are labelled

2.   All bins are lined with reinforced bin liners

3.   Hazardous or flammable liquids are stored correctly

4.   Spillages are dealt with appropriately

5.   Gloves are worn where necessary

6.   Follow storage guidelines/use by dates

Electricity at Work Act 1989

In accordance with the Health and Safety Act, the School ensures the following actions:

1.   Any Exposed wires will be identified an covered where appropriate

2.   Electricity surges due to power overload

3.   Any worn or old sockets to be replaced

4.   A yearly PAT test to be carried out

Data Protection Act 1998

All information must be stored safely and correctly at all times:

1.   Written information to be stored under lock and key for 3 years

2.   If the client wishes to remain anonymous, initials can be used

© The AATT

Swedish Body Massage Course

3. All Computer stored information must be kept for 7 years

4. This must be registered with Data Protection who will issue a personal code for access of records.

5. This allows for securely stored information and access to information on requestSALON CODES OF CONDUCT

- Identify any contra-indications and establish a Treatment Plan with your Client

- Be presentable, clean and tidy

- Protect yourself and your client from cross-infection

- Promote a professional image at all times

- Good communication skills

- Approachable Body language

- Listen to the needs of your client

- Record all information in accordance with the law

- Do not discuss client information

- Always have the appropriate insurance cover

- Ensure the workplace is clean at all times

- Provide fresh towels and covers for each client/student

- Toilet and hand washing facilities available

- Use Antiseptic wet wipes on the feet, and couch roll for them to step onto

- Work place well ventilated

Swedish Body Massage Course

Presentation Of The Therapist

- Have clean and short nails

- Remove jewellery

- Clean uniform

- Flat and comfortable shoe

- Hair tied back

- Appropriate smell on breath and person

- Cover any cuts on hands

Hygiene In The Workplace:

The Three areas are as follows:

Sterilisation- This is the total destruction of all living micro organisms and their spores

Methods would be:

Autoclave- This has a very high steam pressure which heats beyond boiling point. This is a very effective method of sterilisation.

Chemical Liquids- Commonly used are Marvicide and Cidex, tools need to be left in the liquid for 15-20 minutes.

Glass Bead- Small, Glass beads heated to a very high temperature, tools are placed between the beads for only a short period of time.

Sanitisation- This is the destruction of many but not all micro-organisms, and it inhibits any further growth.

Methods are as follows:

UV Cabinet- This is a good place for sterilised tools to be stored in.

© The AATT

Swedish Body Massage Course

Barbicide- This will kill bacteria but not usually the spores. Effective for storing tools during treatments.

Disinfection- This kills micro-organisms but not their spores. They do sustain the level of the micro-organism.

Methods are as follows:

Surgical Spirits- This is a good disinfectant used for wiping tools and surfaces.

Sanitisers- With antiseptic properties, they destroy and prevent the growth of micro-organisms and can be used on the skin.

THE HISTORY OF SWEDISH BODY MASSAGE

Swedish Body massage history dates back to Ancient times and was practised by the Chinese, Greeks and Romans. Historical Records show that body massage was practised in China as early as 3000 B.C.

A Biblical reference from 493 BC documents daily massage for the wives of Xerxes using olive oil and myrrh. It was the ancient Greek philosopher, Aristotle, who argued that physical touch is the most fundamental of all five senses. In the 5th Century B.C., the Greek Physician, Heradosis, used herbs and oils. His pupil, Hippocrates, recognized the benefits of stroking movements toward the heart long before circulation of the blood was discovered. Hippocrates was a physician and is generally regarded as the father of medicine. Hippocrates seems to have understood the benefits of Swedish massage; he used friction movements in the treatment of sprains and dislocations and kneading movements to treat constipation.

Massage has long been known for its beneficial results and allows for most of the body to be massaged and manipulated from the legs, arms, stomach and décolleté to the hands, feet, upper and lower back and the face and scalp.

Effleurage
This massage move is used at the beginning and end of a massage and usually joins other moves together throughout. It is a long, slow rhythmic move that introduces massage to the client and relaxes their muscles in preparation for deeper moves. The pressure should always be firm on the upward stroke and lighten upon the return.

Petrissage
This movement is normally applied with the fingers and balls of the thumbs, and is a deeper move that lifts muscle away from bone, helping contracted muscle to relax.

Percussion
A series of deep, penetrative moves called Hacking, Cupping, Pounding and Plucking. These moves are delivered to deeply stimulate muscle fibres and the increase of blood circulation.

Swedish Body Massage Course

THE BENEFITS OF MASSAGE

The benefits of Swedish Body Massage are countless and range from physical to psychological. It can aid relaxation, depression, anxiety and insomnia to physical benefits such as:

- Relieving aches and pains

- Swollen muscle and joint pain

- Aids blood circulation

- Stimulates the lymphatic system to eliminate waste

- Improve bodily functions

- Helps to maintain health and well-being

- Relieves muscular tension due to the effective removal of toxins from the body

- Fibrous adhesions can be removed

- An overall improvement in muscle tissue

- Improves blood circulation, increasing the distribution of nutrients and oxygen around the body and eliminating carbon dioxide

- Stimulates and calms sensitive nerve endings

- Hyperaemia is increased (blood flow) having a warming effect

- Improves the circulation, nourishing cells and aiding repair

- Aids desquamation (removal of dead skin cells)

- Stimulation of the sebaceous gland- Increases sebum production

- The sudoriferous glands (sweat glands) are stimulating producing perspiration which eliminates the body's waste

- It induces a deep sense of well-being and relaxation

- It energises the client and can have an uplifting effect

- A decrease in stress levels

-

Swedish Body Massage Course

THE CONTRA-INDICATIONS

A Contra-Indication can either prevent or restrict a treatment. In the case of prevention, a Doctor's Note must be provided and a consent signature.

Prevent Treatment

- High or Low blood pressure – may bring on heart attack if high, dizziness and fainting if low.

- Thrombosis and Phlebitis – inflammation of the veins, which may be aggravated by the treatment.

- Recent accidents, injuries or surgery. Scar tissue may re-open.

- Active cancer or other serious medical conditions.

- Life maintaining medication – may affect the response to the medication.

- Diabetes – may change the blood-sugar level. Doctor's note recommended.

- Skin infections or infectious diseases – may spread the condition to other areas of the body.

- Epilepsy – may bring on an attack.

- Under the influence of drugs or alcohol – may become abusive, may fall off the couch and so on.

Restricts Treatment

- Severe bruising, cuts and abrasions. Avoid massage to the area.

- Recent fractures and sprains. Could be uncomfortable for client.

- Asthma & allergies. May aggravate condition.

- Undiagnosed lumps. Should be avoided until diagnose

© The AATT

THE STATE OF HOMEOSTASIS

The body has a natural ability to monitor and maintain its own internal state, providing the right conditions that enable the tissues and organs to function effectively. This process is called Homeostasis.

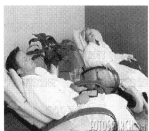

The Hypothalamus controls this automatic process. Health is deemed to be present when all of the bodily functions are in perfect balance and working effectively. Disease then, could be described as the absence of health.

Homeostasis is an ongoing process. If you do not drink enough water during the day for instance, the body will preserve fluids by restricting the activity of the kidneys which in turn restricts elimination of fluids via the urinary system. Another example would be the process of perspiration as a necessary way for the body to cool down and restore its temperature back to normal.

Many holistic practitioners say that all forms of disease stem from a disharmony or dis-ease of the body and mind. It has been suggested that an imbalance both emotionally and physically which has gone untreated for a long length of time can present a form of disease. By the time our sensory nerves tell us there is pain in the area, this is the final warning of an illness that has been present for many months even years before the pain is registered. It is the job of a holistic practitioner to treat each person individually, to treat the whole body not just the problem area, and to treat any imbalances in the body. This will restore harmony and in time homeostasis will return. A good knowledge of Anatomy and Physiology will help you to understand the relationship that the central nervous system plays in the role of stress, arousal, excitement, relaxation and of course, homeostasis.

It is important to establish a good relationship with your client, to put them at ease and make them feel that they can confide in you. To find out their emotional state as well as their physical will allow you to help your client more effectively.

Swedish Body Massage Course

Client Re-Assurance

Due to the fact that a client has to undress for this therapy, you may need to offer more re-assurance than normal. Towel Management is very important to allow the client to keep their modesty.

- Explain clearly to them what they need to take off, how they need to lie on the couch i.e.: face up or face down and hand them a towel to cover up when they have changed. For a back, neck and Shoulder massage, they will only need to take off their top, but trousers must be loose enough to pull down to the coccyx. They may prefer to do this themselves prior to treatment.

- Leave the room, hold a towel up in front of you and them or turn away whilst they undress.

- Only expose an area when it is to be massaged. Then cover and uncover the next area to be massaged.

- If the client feels uncomfortable with an area being massaged, avoid it.

- Make sure that there is no disturbances throughout the treatment- lock the door if necessary.

- Cover the client with two nice clean towels, one for the upper torso, and the other for the lower torso. It will make your towel management easier and allow your client to feel more secure.

- The client must be instructed to remove jewellery, glasses and hair accessories. A plastic bowl should be available to store them.

Swedish Body Massage Course

- Make up will need to be required if the face is to be massaged, which avoids smudging and also allows the therapist to check skin condition. Make up remover should be made available and cotton wool pads.

Client Positioning

The client should be made comfortable with extra support under the ankles or bust if necessary, and a pillow can be given for extra comfort. After establishing a treatment Plan, the client may require the couch to be lowered to get onto it, or they may need help on and off of the couch or to turn over during the massage. Health and Safety Rules should be followed at all times.

Supine- Lying face up- Offer support under head and neck & under knees.

Prone- Face down- Face hole for comfort, support under ankles.

Seated Massage- Appropriate for pregnant clients- Sit them on a stool and lean onto the couch. Pillows & Towels can then be placed on couch. The client should lean forward and rest arms forward.

Creating the right environment

As the client will be undressed during the treatment, the room should be heated to average 23-25 0C. The client should be offered a blanket or quilt for extra warmth. Adequate ventilation should be provided also to prevent cross-infection of diseases or viruses, carbon dioxide and odours.

An ambiance should be achieved by appropriate dimmed lighting and candles, colours, aromas and calming music. Soft furnishings and towels are also a good option.

Blue- This is a healing colour that calms, relaxes and has a soothing effect. It effects the throat chakra and is good for expression and speaking out.

Violet- This is an emotionally calming, deeply relaxing colour that effects the crown chakra which helps the client to really let go.

Swedish Body Massage Course

Yellow- This is a stimulating and uplifting colour which appeals to the solar plexus and is good for clients who lack energy and enthusiasm.

Orange- Once again, it increases energy and sexual levels. It appeals to the sacral chakra and is known to increase appetite.

Red- This increases motivation, grounds us and helps the circulation. It is the colour of the base chakra.

Green- The colour of the heart chakra, this is a nurturing colour which balances, sedates and calms.

MATERIALS REQUIRED

Oil- This should be in a small squeezable container which can be stored in your uniform pocket for ease of application. Contact with the client should not be broken.

Surgical Spirit or Antiseptic Wet Wipes To clean over the feet, trolley and couch.

Plastic Bowl- For cotton wool and jewellery.

Eye Make Up Remover- For removal of the clients make up.

Tissues- For client use and to blot the skin where required.

Couch Roll- To prepare the couch before use.

Towels- Fresh towels must be used to avoid cross infection.

Protective Coverings

- The massage couch should be wiped with surgical spirit and then covered with a special couch cover or two towels. A fitted cover is best because it will not slip. Towels can be added over the massage cover, followed by couch roll. If a pillow is used it must be covered by a towel for hygiene purposes. Towel rolls or bolsters can be used for supporting the knees or feet. Two large towels are recommended for use during the massage.

Swedish Body Massage Course

- If the client has no underwear on paper pants should be provided for hygiene.

- When the client stands on the floor bare foot, a towel with couch roll covering it should be next to them for them to stand on.

- If the client has any skin problems such as athlete's foot, the area should be covered with disposable paper shoes or protective dressing.

- If you have any cuts or abrasions on your hands, you must cover them with protective dressing or wear disposable gloves.

Swedish Body Massage Course

Checking Equipment

- All equipment and materials are clean and hygienic.

- You have plenty of clean towels and linen.

- All products are available and neatly arranged on the trolley in the order that you require them.

- Shower and toilet facilities are clean and in working order

- Sink and water supply is in working order with plenty of soap and paper towels.

- An empty, lined bin should be in the room for waste.

- The massage couch is safe and has clean linen.

- The trolley is wiped down with disinfectant or surgical spirit and has paper protecting it.

Swedish Body Massage Course

CLIENT BREATHING

You should encourage your client to perform deep breathing techniques throughout the treatment. Deep abdominal breathing can be achieved in the following way:

- Breathe using the whole of your chest capacity. Avoid shallow breaths using the upper part of the chest only. Ask the client to take a deep breath in using the whole of their thorax area including the abdomen. Encourage the client to breathe out slowly and controlled. This method will increase the intake of oxygen to the body and helps to induce deep relaxation.

- Any deep tissue work should be applied on the exhale breath, as it will feel much more comfortable for the client.

ESTABLISHING A TREATMENT PLAN

A treatment Plan needs to be established with the client prior to treatment. All details can be recorded on a record card and used for future referral. A treatment plan will include the following:

Medical History- Past and present conditions need to be established and recorded, so that a treatment can be tailor made for the client. It may also affect the way the client is positioned on the couch.

Contra-Indications- They may prevent or restrict the treatment depending on the severity

Contra-Actions- The treatment can be altered according to how the client reacts to the treatment.

Areas to be treated- It may become apparent that a client requires you to concentrate on a specific area and the treatment should be adapted accordingly.

Physical Condition- Look at the clients' skin type and condition, muscle tone, areas of tension, height, size and weight, age, and any other specific problems.

Emotional condition- Discuss whether the client feels stressed, anxious, tense, nervous, depressed and what their energy levels are like.

Posture- Observe the posture of the client. May be due to lifestyle, occupation, driving, carrying small children, heavy shopping, and embarrassment of certain aspect of the body.

Choice of oil- Unless you are a trained Aromatherapist, only a base oil may be applied, which will cater for clients specific needs

Client feedback- This gives important clues as to how to adapt your treatments to maximize effectiveness.

Swedish Body Massage Course

Aftercare Advice- This will determine the effectiveness of the treatment. If a client follows the homecare advice there is much higher likelihood of treatment being successful.

Lifestyle- This plays an important role in their physical and emotional wellbeing. Take into account occupation, relationships, dietary and fluid intake, hobbies, means of relaxation, exercise, social habits such as drinking and smoking, sleep patterns.

Observe The Client

Frowning- They are concentrating or are worried

Hunched Shoulders- They may lack confidence, be embarrassed or upset, may be large busted, or be posturally defective

Wringing- They could be nervous and anxious

Rolling Eyes- This person is exhausted

Lack of eye Contact- A nervous person, may be deceitful or embarrassed

Smiling- A happy, relaxed client

Gesticulating when speaking- There is an empathy and compassion between you.

Swedish Body Massage Course

CONFIDENTIAL CASE HISTORY-SHEET ONE

THERAPISTS NAME_____   DATE/TIME_____

Name_____   Date Of Birth_____

Address_____

Tel No_____   Occupation_____

MEDICAL HISTORY

Physical_____Emotional_____
_____

Name and address of Doctor_____

Medication/Last visit to GP_____

Other therapies receiving & why_____

Relevant Family history of disease_____

Surgical Operations (within 5 years)_____ Allergies___   _____

Menstruation (reg, pain, bloating, moodiness)_____

Pregnancies_____ Menopause_____

Reason for Treatment_____ Other_____

LIFESTYLE/STRESS FACTORS

Smoking_____Drink (tea, coffee, alcohol)_____

Exercise_____ Diet _____

Sleep (reg, waking, refreshed) _____Interests _____

Home Life (settled, stressful)_____Work Life (enjoyable, stressful)___

Anxiety, depression, tension, stress_____   Energy_____

Special needs/likes/dislikes _____

I declare the above information to be correct and consent to the agreed treatment.

Signed _____ Date _____

22

© The AATT

Swedish Body Massage Course

CONSULTATION CASE HISTORY-SHEET TWO

Date_____   Client Name _____

Reactions/Results since last treatment _____

Client Feedback/likes/dislikes/pressure _____

Observations/condition _____

Sensitive Areas of body

Patient reaction during
treatment_____

Sleep Pattern since
treatment_____

Advice
Given_____

Other
Notes/Observations_____

Treatment Plan & Notes for Next Time

_____

Emotional needs (pace & style)

_____

23
© The AATT

AFTER CARE ADVICE

Swedish Body Massage is a very powerful treatment. The circulation is rapidly increased during the massage, and this in turn leads to an increase in nutrition and the way that every single cell in the body functions. With the application of this massage, blood flow is increased through the skin, liver, bowel and kidneys, so detoxification is increased. With Swedish Body Massage, you are accelerating the blood, lymph and digestive fluids in the body. Swedish Body Massage is a profoundly healing therapy. It helps the release of toxic build up or lactic acid due to exercise, and is excellent for sportspeople who need to maximise circulation and health of the body.

During the Treatment

Sleepiness, coughing and sneezing, temperature changes, laughter and tears, increased pain in already painful areas, pain and tingling in the body, light-headedness, headaches, appearance of infection like a cold, changes in emotions, deep relaxation and a meditative state, a sense of release and de-stress.

After the Treatment (within 24 hours)

Increased energy or tiredness, increased bowel or bladder movement, coughing and sneezing, nausea and vomiting, dreaming and changes in pattern of sleep, spots and rashes, laughter and tears, increased pain in already painful areas or recurrence of symptoms, appearance of infection such as a cold, heightened emotions, feeling on top of the world, in an introverted state, clearer state of mind, feeling of being cleansed.

Swedish Body Massage Course

After Care Advice

For maximum effect from your Swedish Body Massage, the following After Care is recommended.

- Drink as much fresh water as possible. This will assist the body in flushing out the toxins that have been released into your system.

- Eat a light meal. Raw foods such as vegetables and fruit are excellent for their cleansing effect.

- Rest as much as possible. This will allow the body to heal.

- Avoid smoking and alcohol.

- Cut down on tea and coffee.

- Rest Well

Avoid all the S's for the next 24 hours:

- Swimming

- Sauna

- Steam Room

- Strenuous Exercise

Swedish Body Massage Course

VARIATIONS IN TREATMENT APPLICATION

Although you will be taught a standard routine, you may be required to adapt your treatment to fit your client's physical and emotional needs:

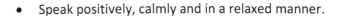

Relaxation

- This would be for a client who is stressed, highly strung or suffers from insomnia.

- Speak positively, calmly and in a relaxed manner.

- Encourage the client to talk about their issues during the consultation.

- Suggest they visualise a relaxing place.

- Privacy needs to be ensured, the right ambience and room temperature a must.

- Encourage the client not to talk throughout the treatment.

- Get your client to practice deep abdominal breathing.

- Use lots of therapeutic touching, linking and effleurage.

- Concentrate on areas of tension such as the shoulders, neck, forehead and eyes.

- Flowing movements with a slow, even pace.

- Maintain contact with your client.

- Hand placement on each chakra is advised.

Swedish Body Massage Course

Uplifting
This would be for a lethargic client who lacks motivation and energy.

- Be upbeat and enthusiastic.

- Apply deeper, penetrative movements.

- Reduce the level of effleurage moves and increase petrissage, pressure points and vibrations.

- The massage should be performed in a more invigorating than normal.

Male Massage
The client should be treated in an equal manner, but the application may need to be varied.

- Specific instructions given when asking the client to prepare for the massage.

- Place one towel widthways across the chest area, a towel folded into a double layer across the lower abdomen and a towel lengthways over the legs.

- Usually larger, deeper moves are required.

- Avoidance of the buttock area may be an option.

- Be aware of the client's space, try not to lean over too close.

- No suggestive comments or innuendo should be given.

Weight
A client's weight should be established in order to check level of fitness. If a client is overweight they may suffer from joint problems, immobility, blood pressure and breathing problems or diabetes. A large client has more adipose tissue which will

Swedish Body Massage Course

require a deeper massage to relax muscular tension. The opposite applies with a client who has a low amount of adipose tissue. Levels of pressure and requirements need to be discussed prior to treatment.

Size

A client's body size must be considered. A larger client may require more strokes to cover the area and the opposite applies for a smaller client. Body size will determine the amount of oil needed to provide slow, smooth strokes. A larger couch may also need to be considered.

Muscle Tone

Muscle tone can vary a lot from client to client. The massage needs to be adapted accordingly to meet the client's needs.

Tension

A client who suffers from tension will have muscles that are hard to touch and which have contracted. The scalp may well feel tight, they may be frowning and often their shoulders are pulled upwards and inwards towards the ears. Extra effleurage and petrissage should be performed to the whole area, as the whole body is usually effected from the tightness of muscles.

Tension Nodules

Predominantly found around the trapezius muscle which runs across the top of the shoulders, along either side of the neck and in between the scapula. Moveable nodules, they slide underneath the fingers when pressure is applied and may click or crunch when manipulated. They are not visible to the eye, and are only detected when touched. Petrissage is the best move for tension nodules.

Muscle Fatigue

This is where a muscle fails to relax resulting in muscle spasm and pain in area. Caused by sustained isometric exercise or insufficient rest periods during exercise, it results in a lack of

Swedish Body Massage Course

oxygen, nutrients and an accumulation of waste products in the muscle, mainly lactic acid. Massage will help to remove lactic acid within the muscle, work deeply and drain toxins away to the nearest lymph nodes.

Advise the client to 'warm up' the muscles sufficiently prior to exercise and to 'stretch out' sufficiently after exercise.

Swedish Body Massage Course

JUDGING THE EFFECTIVENESS OF A SWEDISH BODY MASSAGE

It is helpful to be able to judge the effectiveness of your treatment, as during feed-back many clients will be too kind to speak the truth. As a result of judging yourself, you will be able to read signs for yourself and adapt your techniques accordingly. If you provide a treatment which meets all expectations, this will ensure repeat business and an increase in profits.

You should judge the effectiveness of your treatment from beginning to end, and this can be done by observing the client visually, asking questions at the beginning and the end and asking your client for written feed-back at the end of the treatment. Your methods should be discreet and should not interfere with the treatment. The client should feel that they are being helpful when they give feed-back.

Visual Signs

- Is there any erythema and if so, is it even or patchy as this could point to your application technique or a problem the client is suffering with.

- Do the muscles feel more relaxed

- Was the client relaxed during the treatment

- Did the client feel more alert after the treatment

- Does the clients breathing appear deep and relaxed

- Was the client still or fidgety during the treatment

- Look at the clients body language when they return to reception

Swedish Body Massage Course

Verbal Signs

- Ask them how the massage move feels

- Did they manage to sleep

- How does their skin feel

- Do they feel tension free

- Was there any part of the massage they found uncomfortable

- How is the pressure

- How do they feel they would improve the massage next time

- Did they relax mentally

Written Feed-back

- The clients level of satisfaction

- What were the benefits gained

- The clients reaction overall to the massage

- Therapist performance

THE EFFECTS OF MASSAGE ON BODILY SYSTEMS

Blood Flow And Pulse Rate

When a massage or heat treatment is applied to the body, due to the warmth produced, the blood vessels dilate or widen as they try to cool the body by moving closer to the surface of the skin.

This slows down the speed the blood travels through the arteries which will lower blood pressure. The pulse rate is increased during massage due to the stimulating and warming effect it has on the body's physiology.

The Circulatory System

Massage stimulates the circulation and has a beneficial effect on conditions such as arthritis and joint pain. The application of a massage oil can also help. It enters the blood circulation very quickly after application and can affect the organs as well as bodily functions. Any residue will be eliminated via bodily functions- skin, urine.

Base Oils can also: *Reduce blood pressure, * Increase blood pressure, * Sedate and reduce palpitations, * Increase circulation, * Reduce diameter of blood vessels.

The Nervous System

- Soothes nerve endings if applied in relaxed way

- Stimulates nerve endings if vigorous massage

- Soothing effect on mental activity of brain

- Uplifting effect on mental activity of brain

- Certain massage oils can have: * Calming effect on CNS, *Stimulating and strengthening effect on CNS.

Swedish Body Massage Course

The Lymphatic System

- Aids removal of waste by stimulating lymph fluid

- Drains lymph fluid towards lymph nodes

- Prevents oedema

- Assists treatment of oedema by draining tissue fluid from the area

- Improves appearance of tissues by stimulating Lymphatic system into removing waste and toxins.

- Certain massage oils can: *Stimulate immunity by encouraging production of white blood cells, *Has a diuretic effect which helps increase lymphatic and tissue fluid circulation, preventing oedema, *Increases the absorption of waste materials from the tissues.

Swedish Body Massage Course

The Integumentary System

- Stimulation of the sebaceous glands which maintain natural lubrication of the skin

- Stimulation of the sweat glands to eliminate waste and control body temperature

- Aiding the removal of dead skin cells (desquamation), improving appearance of skin

- Stimulating or soothing effect on the nerve endings

- Increases the circulation of blood supply to skin, nourishing skin cells and helping healthy production

- The warmth produced by massage helps skin to relax, opening pores and hair follicles and increasing the absorption of massage medium

Application of massage oil onto the skin during massage is the most common route of absorption. The oil is absorbed by the skin. Oil is fat-soluble and dissolves into the sebum and into the dermis of the skin. It is then carried into the body via the blood stream and lymph vessels. This process will depend on the thickness/quality of the oil. The benefits can be:

- Oil can regulate the skin by balancing the production of sebum

- Oils can calm and soothe the skin

- Oil can improve the rate of protection, as many oils are anti-bacterial and antiseptic

- Oils can aid skin cell regeneration

Swedish Body Massage Course

The Skeletal System

The bones of the skeleton are effected by massage as the blood supply is increased which brings extra nutrients and minerals to the bones. It will have a lubricating effect on the joints of the bones too as the synovial fluid is stimulated.

Massage Oil can help the skeletal system by:

- Producing anti-inflammatory properties which help reduce inflammation of the joints

- Producing an Analgesic effect which aids relaxation within the ligaments

The Muscular System

- Relieves muscular tension due to removal of wastes/toxins

- Improves blood circulation, increasing amount of nutrients & oxygen being delivered to area improving muscle tone and condition

- Causes hyperaemia(increased blood flow) which has warming effect and helps prevent muscular injury

- Muscle cells receive nourishment which increases cell division and in turn their condition

- Tense or short muscles can be relaxed and stretched, which helps correct postural faults

- Massage oil can remove muscle waste such as lactic acid

- Oil can have analgesic effect bringing relaxation to tense muscle fibres and tendons

Swedish Body Massage Course

THE SKELETAL SYSTEM

Functions

Support

Protection	Skull protects brain
	Rib cage protects heart and lungs
	Vertebral column protects spinal cord
	Pelvic girdle protects lower abdominal viscera
Movement	Bones act as levers with muscles attached joints formed where two or more bones meet
Blood Cell Production	In red bone marrow
Storage	Minerals, particularly calcium and phosphorous, stored in bone and released into blood when needed
	Fat stored in yellow marrow

Classification Of Bones

Long	Bones of limbs (except carpals, tarsals, patella)
Short	Carpals, tarsals
Flat	Skull bones, ribs, sternum, scapulae
Irregular	Vertebrae, facial bones
Sesamoid	Patella

Classification Of Joints

Fibrous	Immovable - e.g. sutures of skull

Swedish Body Massage Course

Cartilaginous	Slightly movable - e.g. between vertebral bodies
Synovial	Freely movable
Ball and Socket	Enables all movements - hip and shoulder
Hinge	Flexion/extension e.g. elbow, knee
Gliding	E.g. between carpals, between tarsals
Condyloid	Flexion/extension, abduction/adduction, e.g. wrist, first knuckle joint
Pivot	Rotation only - e.g. atlas/axis
Saddle	Base of thumb only, flexion/extension, abduction/adduction, circumduction

The Bones of the Skull

The Cranium and the face is made up of 22 bones, 14 facial bones and 8 cranial bones.

The facial bones help us with our facial expressions and support the eyes and teeth. Some of the bone is made of cartilage which is a softer tissue than bone.

The Cranium covers over, supports and covers the brain.

The Eight Bones Of The Cranium

Occipital	This is the lower part of the cranium and has an opening from which the spinal cord passes.
Frontal	This is at the top of the cranium and forms the forehead.
Parietal	There are two which form the sides of the cranium.
Temporal	There are two each side of the cranium above each ear.

Swedish Body Massage Course

Sphenoid — This joins the temporal and frontal bone at the base of the cranium.

Ethmoid — The eye sockets and some of the nasal cavity are formed by this bone.

The Fourteen Bones Of The Face

The Nasal Bone — Two bones which form the bridge of the nose

Zygomatic Arch — Two bones that run across the cheekbones.

Maxilla — Two bones that aid the upper jaw and roof of mouth.

Mandible — This bone forms the upper jaw.

Lacrimal — Two bones which help form the eye sockets.

Palatine — Two bones that form the roof of the mouth.

Vomer — A bone of the inner nose.

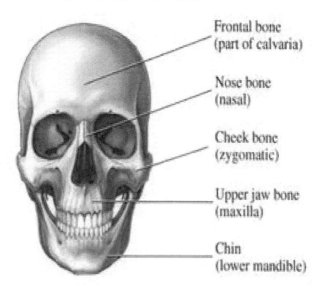

Swedish Body Massage Course

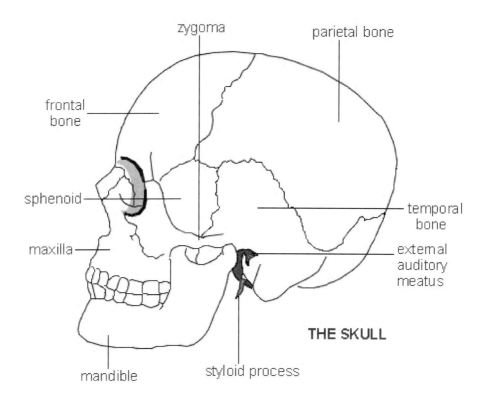

Swedish Body Massage Course

THE MUSCLES OF THE FACE

Sternocleidomastoid
Extends from top of sternum, with a fork to the clavicle, into the mastoid process. Turns the head when one side is in action and tilts head when both sides are working.

Platysma
- Runs along the front and side of the neck.

- Closes the mouth and aids chewing or mastication.

Orbicularis Oris
- Circular muscles around the mouth.

- Closes and compresses lips.

Orbicularis Oculi.
- Circular muscles surrounding the eyes.

- Opens and closes the eyes.

Buccinator
- Main muscle in cheek between upper and lower jaw.

- Compresses cheeks and aids mastication process.

Mentalis
- Muscle of the chin.

- Depresses the lower part of the lip

Masseter
- Jaw Muscle – between zygomatic bone and mandible.

- Opens and closes jaw and gives us the action of chewing.

Risorius
- Runs from angle of mouth across the cheeks.

- Gives us the grinning action.

© The AATT

Swedish Body Massage Course

MUSCLES – ANTERIOR VIEW

Sternocleidomastoid muscle
Omohyoid muscle
Sternohyoid muscle
Trapezius muscle
Deltoid muscle
Pectoralis major muscle
Latissimus dorsi muscle
Serratas anterior muscle
Oblique external muscle
Rectus abdominus muscle

Biceps muscle
Brachialus muscle
Brachioradialus muscle
Pronator teres muscle
Flexor carpi radialus muscle
Palmaris longus muscle
Flexor digitorum superficialus muscle
Flexor carpi ulnaris muscle

Pectineus muscle
Adductor longus muscle
Adductor magnus muscle
Gracilis muscle
Sartorius muscle
Rectus femoris muscle
Vastus medialis muscle
Vastus lateralis muscle

Quadriceps

Peroneus longus muscle
Tibialis anterior muscle
Gastrocnemius muscle
Extensor digitorum longus muscle
Soleus muscle

41
© The AATT

Swedish Body Massage Course

MUSCLES – POSTERIOR VIEW

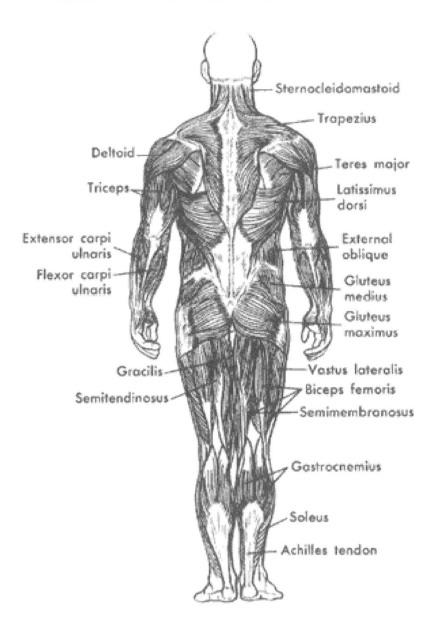

Swedish Body Massage Course

THE RESPIRATORY SYSTEM

Functions

- Takes in oxygen from the air and gets it into the bloodstream.

- Removes carbon-dioxide from the bloodstream and expels it.

- Vital function in forming sound for speech and co-ordination.

Structure

- The Upper respiratory tract

- Mouth, Nose, Sinuses, Pharynx (throat), Larynx (voice box).

- The Lower respiratory tract

- Trachea(windpipe), Bronchi, Lungs - contain Bronchioles and

- Alveoli (air sacs)

The process of respiration

Inspiration

The diaphragm contracts, lengthening the chest cavity, while the external intercostals widen it. This increases the volume of the lungs, causing air to be drawn in to equalize the pressure.

Expiration

The diaphragm and external intercostals relax, decreasing the volume of the chest cavity and lungs which in turn pushes air out. The internal intercostals and other muscles can be used for forced expiration.

Gaseous Exchange

Air is taken in by the nose, filtered, warmed and moistened and then passes through the respiratory tract to its destination- the alveoli of the lungs. Blood capillaries surround the alveoli. The blood extracts the oxygen from the alveoli and passes on carbon dioxide, which is then expelled during expiration. Freshly oxygenated blood returns from the lungs to the heart which then pumps it to all parts of the body.

Swedish Body Massage Course

THE NERVOUS SYSTEM

Structural Division

Central Nervous System (CNS)	The Brain and Spinal Cord
Peripheral Nervous System (PNS)	12 pairs of Cranial Nerves
	31 pairs of Spinal Nerves
	Ganglia (collections of nerve cell bodies outside CNS)

Functional Division

Voluntary NS	Detects Sensation
	Controls movement via skeletal muscles
Involuntary or Autonomic NS processes	Regulates automatic body
	Of heartbeat, respiration, digestion etc via smooth and cardiac muscle and some glands
Subdivided into	
Sympathetic NS	Prepares body for activity in response to stress by:

- Increased heart rate and respiration
- Release of glucose into blood from liver
- Diversion of blood from skin and digestive organs to skeletal muscles
- Sweating
- Dilation of pupils

Swedish Body Massage Course

Parasympathetic NS state	Returns body to relaxed
	Digestive function increases

The Brain

Cerebrum	Receives and interprets Sensations
	Controls voluntary movement
	Seat of memory and conscious thought processes
Cerebellum	Controls muscular co-ordination and balance
Brain Stem	
(Medulla oblongata and Pons varoli)	
	Controls vital functions such as heartbeat, respiration, coughing and vomiting
Hypothalamus	Maintains homeostasis, temperature, water and chemical levels, as well as the autonomic and endocrine functions

Swedish Body Massage Course

DIAGRAM OF THE NERVOUS SYSTEM

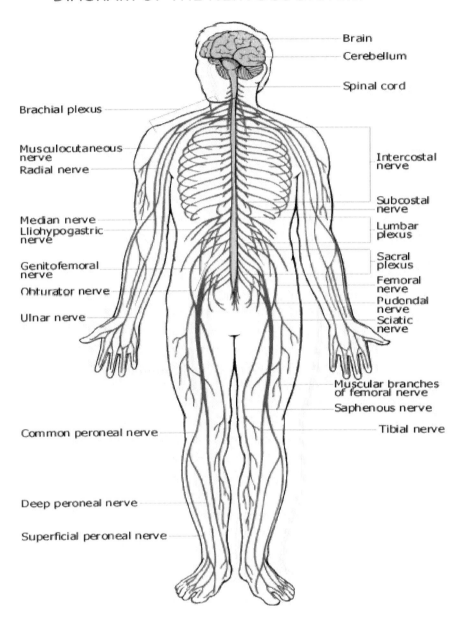

THE CARDIO-VASCULAR SYSTEM

The body's transport system. The heart pumps blood through the blood vessels, which form a network feeding to and from all parts of the body.

The Blood

Plasma (fluid part of blood)

Transports nutrients like glucose and amino acids, firstly from the small intestine to the liver and then from the liver to all body tissues to bring energy, growth and maintenance.

Transports waste products such as urea, away from body tissues to be finally removed by the kidneys or liver.

Transports hormones, enzymes, proteins, ions and gases.

Red Blood Cells (erythrocytes)

Transports oxygen from lungs to body tissues and carbon-dioxide from body tissues to lungs.

White Blood Cells (leukocytes)

Variety of types involved in fighting infection and scavenging dead cell material.

Platelets (thrombocytes)

Involved in blood clotting

Blood Vessels

Arteries

Carry blood away from heart

Carry oxygenated blood, except for pulmonary artery to lungs

Have thick, muscular, elastic walls to help push blood along veins

Return blood to heart

Carry deoxygenated blood, except for pulmonary veins

Have thinner walls and valves to prevent back-flow

Swedish Body Massage Course

Faulty valves can lead to varicose veins

Sluggish flow in legs can lead to blood clotting (deep vein thrombosis)

Capillaries

Arteries and veins linked by networks of capillaries, the smallest blood vessels. Here, body tissues receive oxygen and nutrients from the blood while the blood picks up carbon dioxide and wastes from the tissues.

The Heart

Muscular pump comprising four chambers. Receives deoxygenated blood from all parts of body and oxygenated blood from lungs. Then pumps the deoxygenated blood to lungs and oxygenated blood to all parts of body via the aorta. Heartbeat caused by the closing of valves during pumping. Heart has own blood supply via coronary arteries- blockage by a clot (coronary thrombosis) will cause heart attack.

Swedish Body Massage Course

DIAGRAM OF THE CIRCULATORY SYSTEM

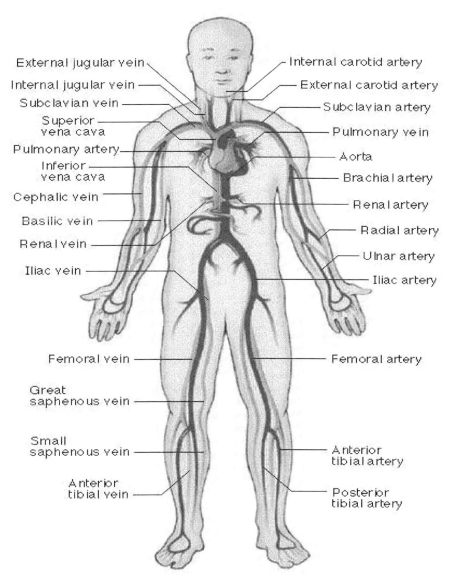

Swedish Body Massage Course

THE DIGESTIVE SYSTEM

The digestive tract or alimentary canal is a muscular tube that extends from the mouth, through the stomach and intestines, to the anus. Its function is to break down food into substances that can be absorbed into the bloodstream and distributed to the body tissues for energy, growth and repair. Peristalsis is the wave like muscular process by which food and waste material are pushed along the digestive tract.

Food Groups

Proteins	From meat, dairy products, pulses and grains
	For growth and repair
	Broken down into amino acids
Carbohydrates	Starches, grains, pulses, root vegetables
	Sugars - sugar, honey, fruit
	Energy foods
	Broken down into simple sugars
Fats (lipids)	From meat, dairy products, oils
	For energy, growth and repair
	Broken down into fatty acids and glycerol
Vitamins and Minerals	Variety found in different foods
	Needed for normal metabolic functions
Roughage (fibre)	Non-digestible material of veg and grains
	Aids peristalsis

Digestive Process

Mouth	Chewing and mixing of food with saliva (begins breakdown of starches)
Oesophagus	Swallowed food pushes towards stomach

Swedish Body Massage Course

Stomach	Mixes food with gastric juices which begin breakdown of proteins and fats and kill bacteria
Duodenum	Received pancreatic juices from pancreas which further break down starches, proteins and fats. Receives bile from gall bladder which further breaks down fats
Small Intestine	Intestinal juices complete breakdown of sugars. Products of digestion absorbed into bloodstream and sent to body tissues via the liver
Large Intestine	Receives undigested food and absorbs water and salts into bloodstream. Remainder excreted via rectum and anus.

Functions of the liver

Receives products of digestion and stores, releases or converts them as required. Stores glycogen, iron and some vitamins. Produces bile - stored in gall bladder. Produces blood plasma proteins- e.g. for clotting. Detoxifies poisonous substances - drugs.

Swedish Body Massage Course

DIAGRAM OF THE DIGESTIVE SYSTEM

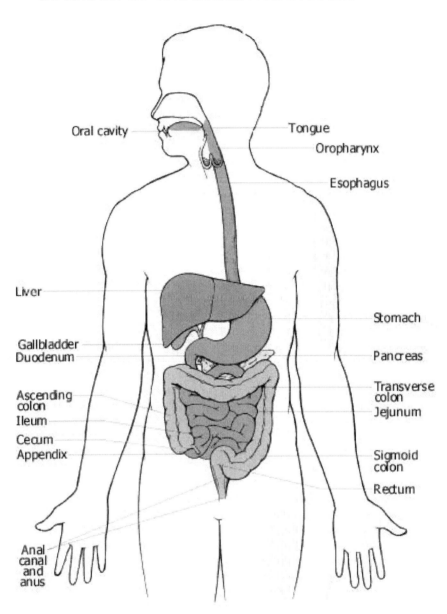

Swedish Body Massage Course

DIAGRAM OF THE SKIN AND THE APPENDAGES

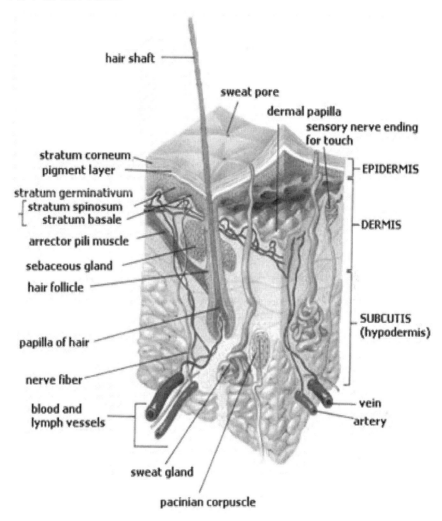

Swedish Body Massage Course

The Seven Main Functions of the Skin are:

Sensation	Detects changes in the environment such as heat, cold, touch and pressure.
Heat Regulation	Helps to regulate the temperature of the body at a constant 37oC by widening and narrowing of blood vessels. Perspiration aids the body in its cooling process and the subcutaneous fat layer helps to insulate the body. The outer temperature is determined by the sensory nerve endings in the dermis.
Absorption	The skin has limited absorption and is waterproof. It allows miner absorption such as with female hormones and facial preparations. About 60% of what is applied to the skin is absorbed.
Protection	A waterproof surface protects the body from dirt, bacterial infection and chemicals. The keratin and the acid mantle both add to the protective layer. The acid mantle is a mix of the sebum and sweat produced in the dermis.
Excretion	The skin excretes waste products through perspiration such as lactic acid, urea and salts.
Secretion	Sebum is secreted by the sebaceous glands.
Vitamin D Production	This occurs due to sunlight on the skin producing a chemical reaction.

Swedish Body Massage Course

The Epidermis- The Upper Layer

The thickness of the epidermis varies in different types of skin. It is thinnest on the eyelids at .05 mm and thickest on the palms and soles at 1.5 mm. The epidermis has no blood vessels or nerve endings.

The epidermis contains 5 layers. From bottom to top the layers are named stratum basale, stratum spinosum, stratum granulosum, stratum licidum, and stratum corneum. The bottom layer, the stratum basale, has cells that are shaped like columns. In this layer the cells divide and push already formed cells into higher layers. As the cells move into the higher layers, they flatten and eventually die. The top layer of the epidermis, the stratum corneum, is made of dead, flat skin cells that shed about every 2 weeks.

Blood vessels in the dermis, below the basale cell layer, supply nutrients to increase the growth of new cells to the surface.

The Stratum corneum (horny layer) is the top layer of the epidermis that we can see.

Stratum Corneum	The horny or outer layer of the skin, it is continuously shedding dead skin cells.
Stratum Lucidum	This is made up of clear, small cells through which light can pass. This layer is only present in the soles of the feet and the palms of the hands.
Stratum Granulosum	The granular layer is 1-3 layers thick, and produces keratin.
Stratum Spinosum	The prickle cell layer is 3-6 layers thick and the cells are constantly dividing.

Stratum Germinativum — A single basal layer of cells containing pigment melanin. The cells of the epidermis are produced in this layer and each has a distinct nuclei. These cells divide constantly with a process called mitosis.

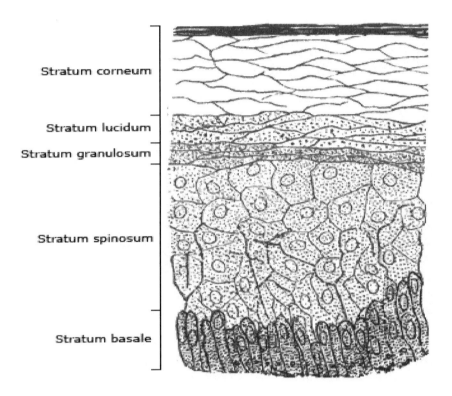

Swedish Body Massage Course

The Dermis- The lower layer

The dermis is the middle layer of the skin located between the epidermis and subcutaneous tissue. The thickest of the skin layers, it comprises a sturdy mesh of collagen and elastin fibres. Both collagen and elastin are critically important skin proteins: collagen is responsible for the structural support and elastin for the resilience of the skin. The cells in the dermis are called fibroblasts, which synthesize collagen, elastin and other structural molecules. The proper function of fibroblasts is highly important for overall skin health. It is important to ensure that the fibroblast is healthy, as it will then produce a healthy cell on the surface of the skin.

The dermis also contains capillaries (tiny blood vessels) and lymph nodes (depots of immune cells). The former are important for oxygenating and nourishing the skin, and the latter -- for protecting it from invading microorganisms.

Finally, the dermis contains sebaceous glands, sweat glands, hair follicles as well as a relatively small number of nerve and muscle cells. Sebaceous glands, located around hair follicles, are of particular importance for skin health as they produce sebum, an oily protective substance that lubricates the skin and hair. When the sebaceous gland produces too little sebum, as is common in older people, the skin becomes excessively dry and more prone to wrinkling. Conversely, overproduction or improper composition of sebum, as is common in adolescents, often leads to acne.

The dermis is the layer responsible for the skin's structural integrity, elasticity and resilience. Wrinkles arise and develop in the dermis. Therefore, an anti-wrinkle treatment has a chance to succeed only if it can reach as deep as the dermis. Typical collagen and elastin creams, for example, never reach the dermis because collagen and elastin molecules are too large to penetrate the epidermis. Hence, contrary to what some

Swedish Body Massage Course

manufacturers of such creams might imply, these creams have little effect on skin wrinkles.

Subcutaneous Fat

Subcutaneous tissue is the innermost layer of the skin located under the dermis and consisting mainly of fat. The predominant type of cells in the subcutaneous tissue is adipocytes or fat cells. Subcutaneous fat acts as a shock absorber and heat insulator, protecting underlying tissues from cold and mechanical trauma. Interestingly, most mammals lack subcutaneous tissue because their fur serves as a shock absorber and heat insulator. Sweat glands and minute muscles attached to hair follicles originate in subcutaneous tissue.

Swedish Body Massage Course

GETTING STARTED

There are certain factors which need to be considered before you set up professionally and charge for your services.

- Get yourself covered with a good complementary therapy insurance policy.

- Wear a uniform. It will make you look more professional and stops you from ruining your own clothes.

- Practice health and hygiene. Always be clean and tidy, tie long hair back, cut your nails and make sure that you haven't overdone the perfume or eaten a garlic dinner beforehand.

- Wash your hands before the treatment and let your customer see you do it.

- Make sure that the treatment area is warm.

- Choose a strong, suitable chair with no wheels and a low enough back to be able to perform all of your strokes.

- Make the environment as relaxing as possible.

- Offer reassurance in order to make your customer feel comfortable with you.

- Avoid chatting during the treatment, as you will not give your best.

- Concentrate on making your treatment as smooth and flowing as possible.

- Be clear about what you are charging, and have details of the treatment available if necessary.

Swedish Body Massage Course

TO BEGIN WITH

- Explain to your client what the treatment consists of, how long it lasts and what is expected of them.

- Check for contra-indications, take a client consultation form and explain after-care. Get their signature of permission.

- Ask them if there is anything in particular that they would like you to focus on, and ask them if they have any questions.

- Tell them that they are expected to undress down to underpants. Either leave the room, or hold a towel up very high whilst they change.

- Explain that they will be expected to lay prone first or vice versa. Check that they are warm enough.

- Allow them to lay back and relax.

Swedish Body Massage Course

MASSAGE MOVES

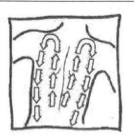	**Effleurage**-A long, continuous and sweeping move, it is performed at the beginning and end of a massage and is used as a connecting stroke during the massage. It introduces touch to the body, warms it up and stimulates the Lymphatic System. Performed in upward strokes toward the heart.
	**Petrissage**-Wringing by applying deeper pressure to lift the underlying tissue and muscle away from bone. The action lifts the skin away, squeezing and releasing it. The tissues are grasped in the palms of the hands and then held between the fingers and the thumbs. Only performed over areas with loose or supple tissue
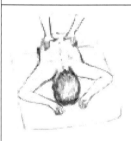	**Petrissage**-To knead using fingers, thumbs or the ulnar border (little finger side of the hand). When performing this move you will use a press and release movement applying pressure similar to that of a pressure point. Depth will depend on area being treated and desired outcome.

Swedish Body Massage Course

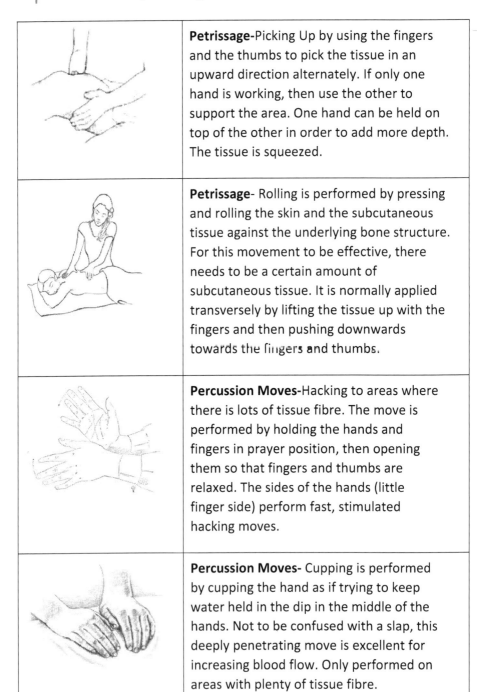

	Petrissage-Picking Up by using the fingers and the thumbs to pick the tissue in an upward direction alternately. If only one hand is working, then use the other to support the area. One hand can be held on top of the other in order to add more depth. The tissue is squeezed.
	Petrissage- Rolling is performed by pressing and rolling the skin and the subcutaneous tissue against the underlying bone structure. For this movement to be effective, there needs to be a certain amount of subcutaneous tissue. It is normally applied transversely by lifting the tissue up with the fingers and then pushing downwards towards the fingers and thumbs.
	Percussion Moves-Hacking to areas where there is lots of tissue fibre. The move is performed by holding the hands and fingers in prayer position, then opening them so that fingers and thumbs are relaxed. The sides of the hands (little finger side) perform fast, stimulated hacking moves.
	Percussion Moves- Cupping is performed by cupping the hand as if trying to keep water held in the dip in the middle of the hands. Not to be confused with a slap, this deeply penetrating move is excellent for increasing blood flow. Only performed on areas with plenty of tissue fibre.

Swedish Body Massage Course

	**Percussion Moves-** Pounding is performed on the lateral edge of the hand with clenched fists. The fist is pounded alternately on an area that is rich in muscle and tissue fibre. Pounding is a fast paced move and not to be confused with a punch. It is a deeply stimulating move.
	**Vibrations-** Shaking may be performed with one hand or both. A similar effect is produced as with the Vibration move, but the movements are much larger and will produce a shaking effect on the muscle. It helps to aid absorption of tissue fluid and can stimulate a sluggish Lymphatic system.
	**Back Stretches-** These can be performed in a horizontal or vertical motion across the back. Hands can perform a stretch and then release. This will loosen up the spinal structure and stimulate nerve endings. A good move to begin and end the massage.

Swedish Body Massage Course

The Routine

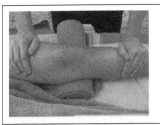	**Application of Oil-**Ensure an even application of oil, One hand above and one hand below the knee avoiding bony protrusions
	**Full Leg Effleurage-**Glide hands at side of lower leg upward. Hands become palm to palm effleurage on upper leg x 6
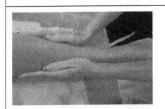	**Lower leg effleurage-** Hands to the side avoiding the tibia, slide them up to below the knee and back down to the ankle x 6
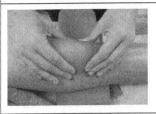	**Massage around the knee-** Using thumbs and fingers gently massage around the patella bone x 6
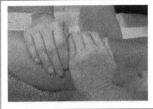	**Upper Leg Effleurage-** Palm to palm effleurage x 6

Swedish Body Massage Course

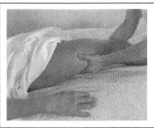	**Petrissage kneading to upper leg and upper outside leg.**- Crab claw motion to upper leg. Anchor hand at ankle, and work up outside leg in kneading x 6
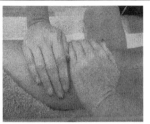	**Upper Leg Effleurage**-Palm to palm effleurage x 6
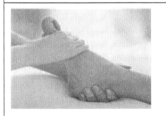	**Leg Stretch**- Perform a gentle leg pull or stretch. Massage the Achilles tendon just above the heel, and pinch each side with thumb and forefinger up the Achilles tendon x 3
	**Massage the front of the feet**- Use thumbs to fan out from middle to outer foot. Run fingers down in a stroking motion in between foot bones x 6
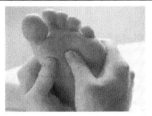	**Massage the underneath of the feet**- Use thumb pressure to massage the underfoot. Use knuckles to work the heel deeply

Swedish Body Massage Course

	**Toe Rotation-**Rotate each toe clockwise and then anti-clockwise. Finish with a gentle pull
	**Full arm effleurage-**Start at the wrist and bring hands up the arm over the shoulder and back down x 6
	**Single hand effleurage-**Hold at the wrist and work inner and then outer arm x 6
	**Circular Massage-**Hold hand and work thumb up outer lower arm in circular motion and repeat on inner lower arm x 6
	**Upper arm effleurage-** Hands side by side or palm to palm, work up and around the shoulder x 6

Swedish Body Massage Course

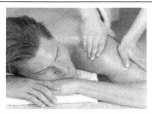	**Petrissage kneading to upper arm-** Continue by anchoring one hand at wrist and kneading to outside upper arm x 6
	**Petrissage kneading under muscle fibres of the shoulder-** Finish with a full arm effleurage
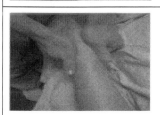	**Open out the hand-** Using heel of hand, open out the wrist and repeat x 6
	**Circular finger petrissage-** Work one side first or both of the face together. Start at forehead in circular motions, then working cheeks and chin area and back up to forehead.
	**Massage the back of the hand-** Using thumbs and knuckles, work the entire hand and finish with a full arm effleurage
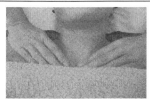	**Effleurage to décolletage, arm, shoulder and neck-** Massage around the shoulder and up to the occipital with a neck pull x 6

Swedish Body Massage Course

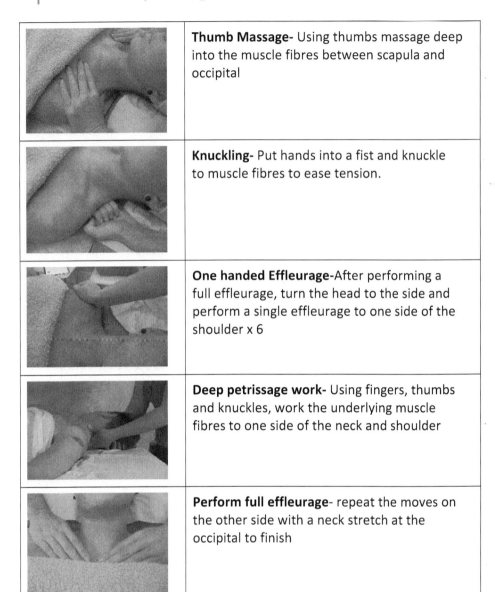

	Thumb Massage- Using thumbs massage deep into the muscle fibres between scapula and occipital
	Knuckling- Put hands into a fist and knuckle to muscle fibres to ease tension.
	One handed Effleurage- After performing a full effleurage, turn the head to the side and perform a single effleurage to one side of the shoulder x 6
	Deep petrissage work- Using fingers, thumbs and knuckles, work the underlying muscle fibres to one side of the neck and shoulder
	Perform full effleurage- repeat the moves on the other side with a neck stretch at the occipital to finish

Swedish Body Massage Course

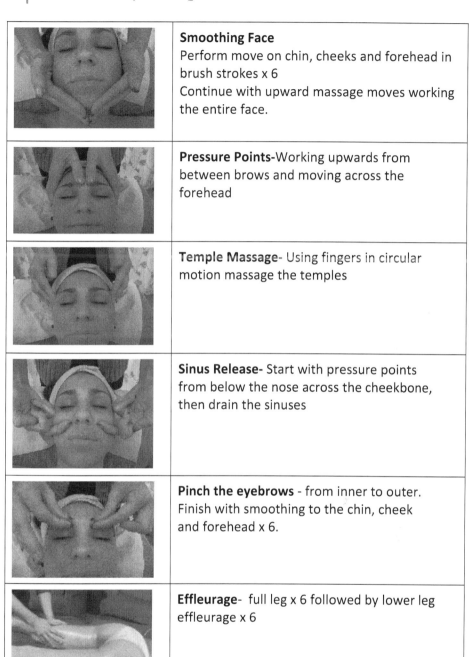

	Smoothing Face Perform move on chin, cheeks and forehead in brush strokes x 6 Continue with upward massage moves working the entire face.
	Pressure Points - Working upwards from between brows and moving across the forehead
	Temple Massage - Using fingers in circular motion massage the temples
	Sinus Release - Start with pressure points from below the nose across the cheekbone, then drain the sinuses
	Pinch the eyebrows - from inner to outer. Finish with smoothing to the chin, cheek and forehead x 6.
	Effleurage - full leg x 6 followed by lower leg effleurage x 6

© The AATT

Swedish Body Massage Course

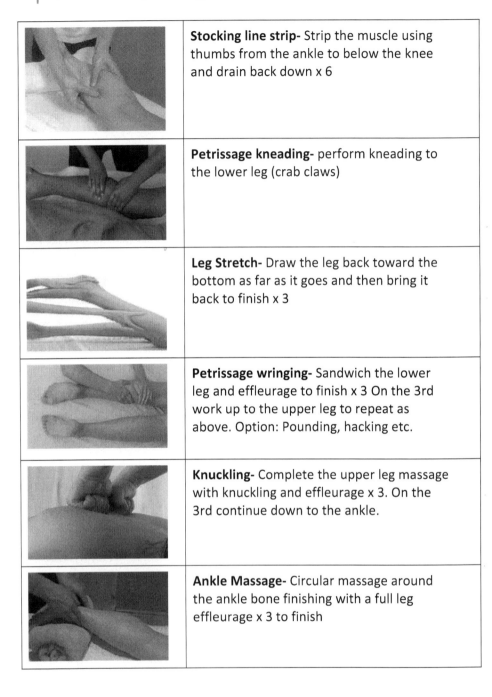

	Stocking line strip- Strip the muscle using thumbs from the ankle to below the knee and drain back down x 6
	Petrissage kneading- perform kneading to the lower leg (crab claws)
	Leg Stretch- Draw the leg back toward the bottom as far as it goes and then bring it back to finish x 3
	Petrissage wringing- Sandwich the lower leg and effleurage to finish x 3 On the 3rd work up to the upper leg to repeat as above. Option: Pounding, hacking etc.
	Knuckling- Complete the upper leg massage with knuckling and effleurage x 3. On the 3rd continue down to the ankle.
	Ankle Massage- Circular massage around the ankle bone finishing with a full leg effleurage x 3 to finish

Swedish Body Massage Course

	Full back effleurage- Moving the hands up the back, around the shoulders and back down x 6. Continue with a single figure of eight starting at the buttock
	Petrissage Kneading- Perform to the full back each side avoiding the spinal column
	Thumb massage to the neck- Glide up to the neck and use circular thumb massage moves just below the occipital.
	Thumb Circling and Pull Back- Work the fleshy area of the lower back and complete the move with a pullback x 6
	Effleurage around the shoulder blade to warm the area
	Deep Petrissage Work- Perform deep moves using fingers, thumbs and knuckles to ease tension
	Palm to Palm Effleurage- Perform effleurage up the back starting at the glutes. Spread thumb and fingers out and work upper muscle x 6

Swedish Body Massage Course

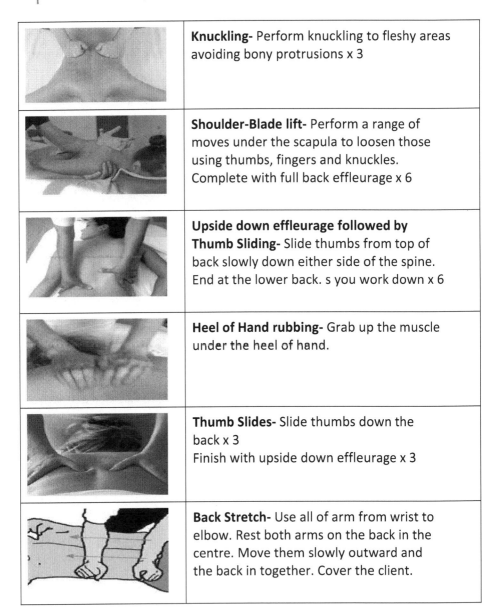

	Knuckling- Perform knuckling to fleshy areas avoiding bony protrusions x 3
	Shoulder-Blade lift- Perform a range of moves under the scapula to loosen those using thumbs, fingers and knuckles. Complete with full back effleurage x 6
	Upside down effleurage followed by Thumb Sliding- Slide thumbs from top of back slowly down either side of the spine. End at the lower back. s you work down x 6
	Heel of Hand rubbing- Grab up the muscle under the heel of hand.
	Thumb Slides- Slide thumbs down the back x 3 Finish with upside down effleurage x 3
	Back Stretch- Use all of arm from wrist to elbow. Rest both arms on the back in the centre. Move them slowly outward and the back in together. Cover the client.

Swedish Body Massage Course

CONTACT DETAILS:

Deborah Jay Kelly
07860 727486
www.deborahjaykelly.com
http://www.angel-academy.co.uk/
https://www.iplandlasercourses.com
https://www.facebook.com/deborah.kelly.7796
www.facebook.com/AngelAcademy info@angel-academy.co.uk
https://twitter.com/TheAngelAcademy
http://www.youtube.com/user/TheAngelAcademy?feature=mhee
https://uk.pinterest.com/deborahkelly779/
https://www.tumblr.com/blog/deborah-j
http://www.starnow.co.uk/deborahjaykelly

AWARDS
Current Mrs Classic British Empire 2017
Winner of 'Best Female Presenter' 2017
LOANI Award for 'Global Ambassador'
'Be It Award' for Woman of Purpose 2016
Nominated 'Best TV Personality' 2016
Nominated 'Best Female Presenter 2016
Nominated 'Female Role Model of the Year' 2016
Winner of 'Best Reality TV Personality 2014
Nominated 'Most Inspirational Woman' 2015
Star Award Winner for Extraordinary Women 2016
Finalist for 'International Face of the Globe'

Best Wishes
Deborah Jay Kelly xxx